Journey
to the
CROSS

A PERSONAL REFLECTION
ON THE COST OF SALVATION

INSIGHT FOR LIVING

DEVOTIONAL

JOURNEY TO THE CROSS
A Personal Reflection on the Cost of Salvation

Journey to the Cross: A Personal Reflection on the Cost of Salvation is from the Bible-teaching ministry of Charles R. Swindoll who has devoted his life to the clear, practical teaching and application of God's Word and His grace. A pastor at heart, Chuck has served as senior pastor to congregations in Texas, Massachusetts, and California. He currently pastors Stonebriar Community Church in Frisco, Texas, but Chuck's listening audience extends far beyond a local church body. As a leading program in Christian broadcasting, *Insight for Living* airs in major Christian radio markets around the world, reaching churched and un-churched people groups in languages they can understand. Chuck's extensive writing ministry has also served the body of Christ worldwide and his leadership as president and now chancellor of Dallas Theological Seminary has helped prepare and equip a new generation for ministry. Chuck and Cynthia, his partner in life and ministry, have four grown children and ten grandchildren.

Journey to the Cross: A Personal Reflection on the Cost of Salvation was written as a reflective devotional by the Creative Ministries Department of Insight for Living. All of the writers are graduates of Dallas Theological Seminary with Master of Theology degrees.

Editor in Chief: Cynthia Swindoll
Director: Mark Gaither
Editors: Greg Smith, Amy Snedaker
Copy Editors: Brie Engeler, Mike Penn
Cover Designer: Joe Casas

Unless otherwise identified, Scripture references used in this book are from the New American Standard Bible®, Copyright © 1960, 1962, 1963, 1968, 1971, 1972, 1973, 1975, 1977, 1995 by The Lockman Foundation. Used by permission. (www.lockman.org).

Scripture references identified (THE MESSAGE) were taken from *The Message* by Eugene H. Peterson, Copyright © 1993, 1994, 1995, 1996, 2000, 2001, 2002. Used by permission of NavPress Publishing Group. All rights reserved.

Scripture references identified (NIV) were taken from the HOLY BIBLE, NEW INTERNATIONAL VERSION®. Copyright © 1973, 1978, 1984 by International Bible Society. Used by permission of Zondervan Publishing House. All rights reserved.

An effort has been made to locate sources and obtain permissions where necessary for the quotations used in this book. In the event of any unintentional omission, a modification will gladly be incorporated in future printings.

Cover Image: Copyright © 2005 William J. Hebert/Stone

ISBN: 1-57972-668-2

Printed in the United States of America

Journey
to the CROSS

A PERSONAL REFLECTION ON THE COST OF SALVATION

*This journal records the
personal conversations between God and*

_____

YOUR NAME

Dear Friend,

As you ushered in the New Year, I would imagine that you made a few resolutions. Perhaps you resolved to pray more, to exercise more often, to save more money, to sign up for those classes you've been meaning to take, to join a Bible study, to start journaling, to work fewer hours so you can spend more time with your family, to get organized . . . the list goes on and on! I admit to making some resolutions myself, some of which I probably will keep more consistently than others.

We make resolutions because, deep down, we believe that by doing certain things, we can improve ourselves. Yet our tendency is to spend so much time focusing on who *we* want to be that we fail to ask ourselves, "Who does *God* want me to be?" As the days flash by and winter melts into spring, our well-meaning resolutions will likely fade, too. Could it be that we're trying to change our attitudes and actions in our own strength without allowing God to change our hearts?

Pastor and author Eugene Peterson writes, "Busyness is the enemy of spirituality. It is essentially laziness. It is doing the easy thing instead of the hard thing. It is filling our time with our own actions instead of paying attention to God's actions."

The season of reflection and preparation leading to Easter offers us an ideal opportunity to combat our spiritual laziness by quieting our hearts and thanking God for the sacrifice He made by sending His Son to earth to die for our sins. I hope you'll take this opportunity to do the "hard thing" by tuning out the deafening noise of everyday life so you can reflect, pray, and, even more importantly, listen to the still, small voice of the Spirit of God.

This book provides you with forty-seven brief but meaningful devotions to reflect on Easter—the single most significant day of celebration for Christians. If one of your resolutions this year is to be drawn into a deeper, more intimate relationship with Christ by knowing Him better through the fellowship of His sufferings, you're holding the right tool in your hands. This book will guide you day by day as it deepens your walk with Him step by step. I pray that our Savior will reveal fresh insights to you as you join me in this passionate journey to the Cross.

Joining you in personal reflection,

Chuck

Charles R. Swindoll

How to Use the Devotional Journal

If you've never used a devotional journal, you may wonder how to start. It's easy, really. Find a place that is quiet and free of distraction, and begin with a short prayer asking the Lord to use the time to teach you. Open the devotional to the appropriate day, and read the inspirational thought and accompanying Scripture passage. Then, after reflecting on what you just read, put your pen to the paper and write the very first words that come to mind. Most likely, they won't be very profound. That's okay. No one needs to see it but you. Just write. After all, this is an exercise in which the process, not the product, is the most important result. Pour your thoughts onto paper without concern for grammar, spelling, or punctuation; without worry or apology; without thinking about how it will read later. Write until you feel a natural point of completion and conclude with a prayer.

A journal is a tool to help you make the best use of your solitude. Some days you will write quite a lot, and you'll be searching for extra scraps of paper. Other days your response will yield only a few words. And like any new venture, it will feel awkward at first. Don't let that stop you. It may be a couple of weeks before you sense the benefit of journaling. If you are like most, you will begin to feel like something is missing from the day when you haven't had this time of reflection.

We hope you will enjoy this journey. May the Lord draw you nearer to Himself and deepen your intimacy with Him as you reflect on the terrible ordeal of the Cross—God's ultimate expression of love for you.

Ash Wednesday marks the beginning of a time-honored period of spiritual reflection and preparation leading up to Good Friday and Easter. This day is called Ash Wednesday because, in some traditions, worshipers kneel to receive an ashen mark drawn in the shape of a cross on their foreheads. The mark is a sign of Christ's ownership of the person and a symbol of sorrow for sins.

Most Protestants don't observe this tradition, but we would do well to reflect on the symbolism. We are His possessions and a true appreciation for the cost of salvation begins with an understanding of the seriousness of sin.

For us, the journey to the Cross begins on this day.

> He himself bore our sins in His body on the cross, so that we might die to sin and live to righteousness; for by His wounds you were healed.

> —1 Peter 2:24

My Father, I kneel before You in thanksgiving for the mark of Jesus Christ on my heart. I am His and He is mine. Without Your salvation, I would have no hope. As I take this journey, reveal the deeper meaning of Your suffering, and with Your touch bring healing to my soul. Amen.

If you're feeling the sting of rejection or the pain of suffering, be encouraged by the knowledge that Jesus has been there too. Throughout His life, He plumbed the depths of sorrow, loneliness, and pain. Physically, Christ was so disfigured at the hands of His torturers that His appearance repulsed people and caused them to look away. The prophet Isaiah wrote:

> He was despised and forsaken of men,
> A man of sorrows and acquainted with grief;
> And like one from whom men hide their face
> He was despised, and we did not esteem Him.
>
> —Isaiah 53:3

Dear Father, It's sometimes hard to accept that Your Son went through so much pain and suffering on my behalf. Lord, thank You for loving me enough to send Your Son to die for me. Thank You that Jesus knew grief and that He completely understands my fears and failings when I am rejected and despised. Allow me to experience more of Your love each day and to share it with others. Help me to glean wisdom and grace from Your Word today and to apply it to my life. Amen.

day 3

Jesus didn't just heal illnesses of the body; He also soothed the infirmities of the soul. His healing ministry on earth foreshadowed His greater spiritual ministry, which culminated at the Cross. The "Suffering Servant," as Jesus is known in the book of Isaiah, carried all the sin and spiritual anguish of the world on His shoulders. When He was crucified, most people in Israel thought He deserved it because He had claimed to be God, which they considered blasphemy. But, in reality, Christ bore the judgment that our sin required:

> Surely our griefs He Himself bore,
> And our sorrows He carried;
> Yet we ourselves esteemed Him stricken,
> Smitten of God, and afflicted.

—Isaiah 53:4

_____

_____

_____

_____

_____

_____

_____

_____

_____

_____

_____

_____

_____

_____

Dear Father, Thank You for sending Your beloved Son, Jesus, to carry my sorrows. Help me today to understand the enormous significance of the sacrifice that He made for me on the cross. When I feel burdened by the weight of life's problems, please help me to trust in Your deliverance as I cast my burdens on You. Give me the faith and perseverance to overcome every obstacle in my path. Teach me the important life lessons that only come through suffering, and help me to keep my eyes on You. Amen.

day 4

We all have been wounded at some time or another—physically, emotionally, or spiritually. We associate our wounds with sorrow and pain. But we can associate Jesus's wounds with the joy of our salvation, because through His suffering we are healed. Jesus experienced acute physical agony, yet He acted in obedience to the Father, even to the point of death. His sacrifice on the cross satisfied the wrath of God against sin. Our heavenly Father forgives us today because each of our transgressions has been paid for once for all by Christ. Isaiah wrote:

> But He was pierced through for our transgressions,
> He was crushed for our iniquities;
> The chastening for our well-being fell upon Him,
> And by His scourging we are healed.
>
> —Isaiah 53:5

_____

_____

_____

_____

_____

_____

_____

_____

_____

_____

_____

_____

_____

_____

_____

_____

_____

_____

_____

_____

Dear Heavenly Father, I am humbled that You crushed Your Son to spare me from eternal death and to heal me of the disease of sin. I am amazed that You believe reconciliation with me was worth the sorrow You and Your Son endured. Help me to remember the great cost of my salvation. I pray that my every thought and deed will show gratitude for the awful price You paid. Amen.

In *The Passion of the Christ*, director Mel Gibson plays a cameo role as one of the soldiers hammering the nails into Jesus's hands. In an interview, Gibson explained, "My sins were the first to nail Him to the cross." It is healthy for us to consider that our own sins personally nailed Jesus to the cross. Doing so reminds us of the pit from which we have been saved and how much grace God has shown us individually. The Father laid our own sins on His very own Son.

> All of us like sheep have gone astray,
> Each of us has turned to his own way;
> But the Lord has caused the iniquity of us all
> To fall on Him.
>
> —Isaiah 53:6

My Father, I am amazed at the grace You demonstrated to save a wretch like me. I was like a sheep going its own way, unconcerned that I had turned my back on You and Your righteous path. I lived only for myself, indulging my sinful desires, ignoring the One to whom I owed my very existence. Thank You, Father—dare I say it?—thank You for laying my own sin on Your own Son. He was—and is—my only hope for all eternity. What amazing grace! Amen.

day 6

It's hard to keep quiet when we are criticized or falsely accused. But that's exactly what Jesus did when the chief priests, scribes, and elders questioned Him and accused Him of blasphemy. He knew that His purpose was to die for the sins of mankind, and He did it willingly, submitting Himself completely to the will of His Father. What amazing love He has for us! We read in Isaiah:

> He was oppressed and He was afflicted,
> Yet He did not open His mouth;
> Like a lamb that is led to slaughter,
> And like a sheep that is silent before its shearers,
> So He did not open His mouth.
>
> —Isaiah 53:7

My Father, Thank You for Your presence in my life. Fill me with Your peace when I face trials, struggles, and uncertainties. Help me to be submissive to Your will just as Jesus obediently submitted to You in love, even when it meant a cruel death on the cross. Give me strength to face each new day with Your power and to stand with confidence upon Your truth. Teach me to trust You when times are hard and to respond in love when I am misunderstood or falsely accused. Amen.

Do you know that our heavenly Father was *pleased* to crush His own Son so that He might add you to His family? Certainly sending His Son to die anguished the Father, but Scripture uses the term *pleased*. The Hebrew word is most often translated *delighted*. This seems strangely malicious for a God of love, doesn't it? Indeed, this would be cruel were it not God Himself, in the Person of the Son, being crushed. God, in the Persons of the Father and the Son, endured this grief for the pleasure of having you as His child.

> But the Lord was pleased
> To crush Him, putting Him to grief;
> If He would render Himself as a guilt offering,
> He will see His offspring, . . .
>
> —Isaiah 53:10

My Father, I am amazed at the extent of Your love for me. You were _pleased_ to put your own Son to death so you could adopt me as Your child. You had spent eternity past in unbroken fellowship with your Son. Because of what You gave, I have now been brought into that eternal fellowship of love. Open my eyes to see the depths of Your love for me that I might be filled to overflowing with You. Amen.

day 8

You've probably heard the common Sunday-school definition of the word *justified*— "just as if I'd never sinned." That definition fails to appreciate the magnitude of this theological term. Sin is an affront to God's holy, righteous nature. Sin is willful rebellion against God, whose character demands punishment for sin. If He were merely to excuse our sin, He would be admitting that He didn't take it very seriously after all. To excuse sin without punishment would be to mock His own character. Through His death, burial, and resurrection, Christ satisfied the demands of God's righteousness on our behalf. By bearing our iniquities, Jesus declares us righteous before our Father. He justified those who have accepted His sacrifice. Isaiah wrote:

> As a result of the anguish of His soul,
> He will see it and be satisfied;
> By His knowledge the Righteous One,
> My Servant, will justify the many,
> As He will bear their iniquities.
>
> —Isaiah 53:11

_____

_____

_____

_____

_____

_____

_____

_____

_____

_____

_____

_____

_____

_____

_____

_____

Dear Father, I thank You today for sending Your Son, the Righteous One, to pay my debt for sin on the cross in order to give me a right standing before You. I'm so grateful that He satisfied the demands of Your holiness and righteousness in my place. Grant me a greater comprehension of Your holy character, so that I may more fully appreciate what it means to be justified. Amen.

When you hear the word *service,* what do you immediately think of? A waiter at a restaurant, community work, or a valet? For the Christ-follower, *service* involves sacrifice. The service we offer others is a powerful, tangible outworking of our faith. Jesus, the One who deserved to be served more than anyone, did not demand service; instead, *He served others.* Jesus acknowledged,

> " . . . just as the Son of Man did not come to be served, but to serve, and to give His life a ransom for many."

> —Matthew 20:28

_____

_____

_____

_____

_____

_____

_____

_____

_____

_____

_____

Father, Thank You today for sending Your Son to model sacrificial service. Teach me to express Your love through serving others, to consider them more important than myself and to lay aside my earthly desires in favor of a greater purpose. Train my heart to desire You so that, by my actions, I can say "I do not come to be served, but to serve." Amen.

day 10

Imagine coming home, only to have your family reject you and throw you out onto the street. God understands rejection—not in theory, but by personal experience. God Himself became a man and presented Himself in the temple—His house. But the religious leaders, those supposedly representing God, accused that very God of sin and murdered Him.

> And He began to teach them that the Son of Man must suffer many things and be rejected by the elders and the chief priests and the scribes, and be killed, and after three days rise again.

> —Mark 8:31

_____

_____

_____

_____

_____

_____

_____

_____

_____

_____

_____

_____

_____

_____

_____

_____

_____

_____

_____

_____

_____

_____

_____

_____

Lord, You know what it feels like to be rejected. It hurts so much when I experience rejection from those who are important to me, and I know that I will be rejected many more times. Use the sting of rejection that I have experienced to help me better understand the sorrow You endured and to identify with Your suffering. Amen.

day 11

Think of the sin in the world. All the sin—the hatred, the bitterness, the envy, the coveting, the murder, the wars, the lying, the deceit, the abuse, the lust, and the pride. Envision six billion people's sin. Multiply it by thousands of years. Now, think of one man piling all of that sin upon himself and taking it all away: its punishment, its guilt, and, ultimately, its presence forever. That's what Jesus came and did. No wonder John the Baptist exclaimed in amazement:

"Behold, the Lamb of God who takes away the sin of the world!"

—John 1:29

Lord, What You accomplished at the Cross is beyond my understanding. How could every sin of every person who ever lived be placed on You? And yet it was. You are the sacrificial Lamb that was slain, the One God sent to bear all of our sins—all of my sins. You were the precious Son the Father gave up, that I might become His precious child. To You be the glory, praise, and thanks forever and ever. Amen.

In Numbers 21:4–9, the Hebrews complained yet again in the Sinai wilderness. In response to their continual rebellion, God sent poisonous snakes as a judgment. Many died. When the people confessed their sins, God told Moses to make a bronze snake and set it up high. Everyone who merely looked at the snake was healed. One trusting look brought God's mercy. God could not have made salvation simpler! In John 3:14–15, Jesus drew this comparison:

> "As Moses lifted up the serpent in the wilderness, even so must the Son of Man be lifted up; so that whoever believes will in Him have eternal life."

_____

_____

_____

_____

_____

_____

_____

_____

_____

_____

_____

_____

_____

_____

_____

_____

Father, You have made salvation so simple. Even a young child can receive eternal life by just looking to Jesus and trusting Him. Let me be one to point others to look upon You. Make my life an uncomplicated, faithful reflection of you so that others might believe. Amen.

Sacrifice. One object surrendered in exchange for another. We may sacrifice short-term satisfaction to gain long-lasting fulfillment. We might even give up something we treasure for the sake of a noble cause. But sacrifice in its fullest sense was realized at the Cross. Jesus Christ chose to surrender His life so that you and I might have a restored relationship with God.

> "This is how much God loved the world: He gave his Son, his one and only Son. And this is why: so that no one need be destroyed; by believing in him, anyone can have a whole and lasting life."
>
> —John 3:16 (THE MESSAGE)

Father, Thank you for loving me so deeply that You sacrificed Your precious Son. You did so willingly, wanting a relationship with me. Your love and tenderness renew my own conviction to surrender to Your authority. I rest in Jesus Christ, trusting in His payment for my sins. I'm so grateful He has purchased eternal life for me. Amen.

A common historical perspective of the crucifixion proposes that Jesus suffered a brutal death at the hands of political rivals. But, in reality, He was wholly God and could have crushed His enemies with a mere thought. Jesus calls Himself the Good Shepherd, willing to give up even His life for those He loved—us, His sheep. The cross and the villains who hung the Savior on it were merely means to an end: atonement.

> "I am the good shepherd; the good shepherd lays down His life for the sheep. . . . No one has taken it away from Me, but I lay it down on My own initiative."
>
> —John 10:11, 18

Father, I praise you for Christ's intentional choice to lay down His life for me. That ultimate act of love prompts me to bow before you in adoration. While He is righteous, powerful, and holy, He is also the tender Shepherd who cares for His flock. May my life reflect such selfless love, as I lay down my own will and instead choose His. Amen.

day 15

On the day of Christ's crucifixion, godless men gloated over the murder of Jesus. But God would have the first and last word. They must have felt foolish when God revealed that their schemes were nothing more than predetermined, foreknown plans of the One they hoped to destroy. From the day the first man committed the first sin, God planned the death of death.

> "This Man, delivered over by the predetermined plan and foreknowledge of God, you nailed to a cross by the hands of godless men and put Him to death. But God raised Him up again, putting an end to the agony of death, since it was impossible for Him to be held in its power."
>
> —Acts 2:23–24

_____

_____

_____

_____

_____

_____

_____

_____

_____

_____

_____

_____

_____

_____

_____

_____

_____

_____

_____

_____

_____

_____

_____

_____

_____

_____

_____

_____

_____

_____

Father, I praise You for overcoming death by the death of Your Son. How ingenious was Your plan. Thank You for making it possible for me to have life. Lord, teach me never to fear anything but You. Amen.

Most people in Jerusalem assumed that Jesus's crucifixion was His end. Yet Peter had startlingly different news on the day of Pentecost—the One they thought dead was now living, even though He had been crucified! This astonishing news led Peter to declare without hesitation: all people can know, without a doubt, that Jesus, God incarnate, is the Messiah who has been promised.

> "Therefore let all the house of Israel know for certain that God has made Him both Lord and Christ—this Jesus whom you crucified."

> —Acts 2:36

_____

_____

_____

_____

_____

_____

_____

_____

_____

_____

Dear Heavenly Father, Many years ago, Peter knew with unparalleled certainty that Jesus was the One who had been promised. This certainty prompted him to declare to anyone who might listen the good news of Jesus the Savior. Today I want to walk with the confidence that Peter had. I pray that I might be filled with the wondrous conviction of Peter, and that his words of good news might pour from my lips to all who need to hear. Amen.

day 17

Given the choice to free either a known killer or Jesus, the people chose the criminal (see Matthew 27:15–25). Our tendency may be to cluck our tongues and wag our heads. *How unjust! How foolish!* Why? Perhaps because we consider ourselves more worthy of mercy than the violent rogue, Barabbas. But consider this: When we accept the gift of life that comes by His death, exchanging our guilt for His innocence, we take our place beside Barabbas. The grace we receive is no less amazing than his.

> "But you disowned the Holy and Righteous One and asked for a murderer to be granted to you, but put to death the Prince of life, the one whom God raised from the dead, a fact to which we are witnesses."

> —Acts 3:14–15

_____

_____

_____

_____

_____

_____

_____

_____

_____

_____

_____

_____

_____

_____

_____

Dear Heavenly Father, I am humbled to realize that I am the freed criminal, while my Lord and Savior was the one crucified. The injustice astounds me, and Your grace in sparing me brings me to my knees. Today, I bow down and rejoice in my new life, granted to me through Your Son's death and resurrection. When I am tempted to be critical or judgmental of others, train my heart to be grateful—for both of us. Amen.

Let's face it. *Religion* is just another form of self-sufficiency—an attempt to treat God like a cosmic vending machine. Appease Him with the right words, right sacrifices, and right incantations, He will conveniently dispense the solution to any particular problem. When Jesus came to the temple, He didn't bring with Him more religious solutions—a cosmic business transaction—He offered Himself, a relationship. This made no sense to the architects of religion. And so they rejected Him.

What about you? Do you want a religion or a relationship? Be careful with your answer. The implications are more far-reaching than you can imagine!

> "He is the stone which was rejected by you [the religious rulers of Israel], the builders, but which became the chief corner stone. And there is salvation in no one else; for there is no other name under heaven that has been given among men by which we must be saved."
>
> —Acts 4:11–12

When God chose to communicate His love to humanity, He spoke in a manner that all could understand. Writing His love letter in His own blood, He spoke to the deepest needs in every human heart, saying, "I love you. I made you. I want to have a relationship with you forever. I died to bring you back to Me." As you consider the Cross today, consider how much God loves you personally, how completely He accepts you, and how pleased He is to have you, because of His own blood shed for you.

> "Be on guard for yourselves and for all the flock, among which the Holy
> Spirit has made you overseers, to shepherd the church of God which
> He purchased with His own blood."

> —Acts 20:28

Lord, Your blood at Calvary has settled forever the question of whether or not I am loved. Not only did You die for me, but You have offered me the gift of eternal life. By faith, I accept the gift of life everlasting with You, and abundant life today from You. Amen.

Do you know that at the Cross Jesus Christ did more than deliver us from the penalty of sin? He also delivered us from the power of sin. By going to the cross, Jesus put Himself under sin's dominion. He *became* sin for us (2 Corinthians 5:21). Under sin's dominion, Jesus was also subject to death's power. But when Jesus died, then rose from the dead, sin's authority over Him ended. He conquered sin and death forever.

> For the death that He [Christ] died, He died to sin once for all; but the
> life that He lives, He lives to God.
>
> —Romans 6:10

As believers, we were joined to Jesus in His death and resurrection (Romans 6:3–5). What happened to Him, happened to us. When He died on the cross, our old self died with Him. When He rose, our new self rose with Him. And we rose just as He did: conquerors over both sin and death. In Christ, we have been freed from sin's rule in our lives.

> Knowing this, that our old self was crucified with Him, in order that
> our body of sin might be [made powerless], so that we would no longer
> be slaves to sin; for he who has died is freed from sin.
>
> —Romans 6:6–7

_____

_____

_____

_____

_____

My Father, I don't look like I have been freed from sin's power. I know at times I don't act like it. But You say that I have been set free from sin's control. Grant me grace to walk in the truth of my freedom in Christ and to depend upon the One who lives within me, for He always lives unto You. Amen.

day 21

Great people do great things. They win friends and influence people. They climb the corporate ladder. They don't humiliate themselves, they don't fight battles that look hopeless, and they certainly don't get themselves killed for no apparent reason.

Jesus, the God-man, challenges all our assumptions about great people. He rejected popularity. He snubbed wealth. He refused to pursue worldly success. He deliberately avoided everything we expect of great men, though He could have had everything and done anything He wanted. But that's not why He came. He came to be humiliated, beaten, and executed like a common criminal. Sounds foolish, doesn't it? Maybe we're fools to follow someone who gained so little and lost so much. Or maybe He wasn't crazy. For through the weakness and foolishness of the Cross came the wisdom and power of God, which is able to save us from something far worse than poverty and offer us something far better than riches. His loss became our gain.

> For the word of the cross is foolishness to those who are perishing, but to us who are being saved it is the power of God.

> —1 Corinthians 1:18

Lord, Thank you for losing so much and looking like a fool in front of the whole world so that I could gain eternal life with You. Thank you for forsaking what was rightfully Yours and coming as a humble servant to give Your life for me. May Your love flow through my life to those in need of You today. Amen.

Sometimes we have to trust Him; we just have to take Him at His Word. Other times, though, He gives us that little bit of evidence—that little bit of proof—that encourages us to keep going a little longer.

When we look back at the death and resurrection of Jesus Christ, the world tries to convince us either that Jesus was alive after the Cross because He never died in the first place, or that Jesus did die on the cross and His body is still in the grave. God, on the other hand, tells us that "Christ died for our sins *according to the Scriptures*," and that "He was raised on the third day *according to the Scriptures*" (emphasis added). As Paul wrote:

> For I delivered to you as of first importance what I also received, that Christ died for our sins according to the Scriptures, and that He was buried, and that He was raised on the third day according to the Scriptures, and that He appeared to Cephas, then to the twelve.
>
> —1 Corinthians 15:3–5

Sometimes that's enough. We take God at His Word and believe that Jesus really died and rose from the dead. But God doesn't stop there. He gives us that extra little bit of evidence that gives our faith a boost. "He was buried." That's the evidence that He really died. "He appeared to Peter, then to the twelve." That's the evidence that He really rose from the dead.

God knows our limitations. He knows that sometimes we are weak and we need a little bit of evidence to strengthen our faith. That's why He provided a tomb as a testimony to Jesus's death and Jesus's post-resurrection appearances—and the changed lives of the apostles—as testimonies of His resurrection.

_____

_____

_____

Father, When I'm at the end of my rope and need perspective, You are always there to provide it at the right time and in the right way. Thank you for understanding my weaknesses and putting my doubts to rest with proof of Your power over death. Because Your Son lives, I have hope of eternal life. Amen.

What has the blood sacrifice of the Lord Jesus accomplished? Before the death of Jesus, non-Jews were not permitted in the inner courts of the Temple to worship the true God. Jews and Gentiles were separated both physically and spiritually. Through faith in Jesus, peace is now available for all who worship the true God of the Bible. The wall of separation has been torn down. All hostility is gone. We are all one in Jesus Christ. We have peace with God and with one another.

> But now in Christ Jesus you who formerly were far off have been brought near by the blood of Christ. For He Himself is our peace.
>
> —Ephesians 2:13–14

_____

_____

_____

_____

_____

_____

_____

_____

_____

_____

Dear Heavenly Father, Thank You that Jesus Christ has made a way for all who worship You to be one. May my heart rejoice in the peace that Your Son has provided me and all true believers. Through all I do and say, make me an instrument of Your peace. Amen.

day 24

The Lord Jesus always existed with the Father and the Holy Spirit. At a point in time, He took on human flesh to become fully human without relinquishing any of His deity. Why? His blood as the God-man was necessary to remove mankind's sin. He could have remained comfortably in heaven and allowed mankind to suffer eternal damnation. Nothing of His righteousness would have been compromised. Yet for the love of us, He chose humility over privilege—He chose to love us more than Himself.

> . . . who, although He existed in the form of God, did not regard equality with God a thing to be grasped, but emptied Himself, taking the form of a bond-servant, and being made in the likeness of men. Being found in appearance as a man, He humbled Himself by becoming obedient to the point of death, even death on a cross.
>
> —Philippians 2:6–8

_____

_____

_____

_____

_____

_____

_____

_____

_____

_____

_____

_____

Lord, You were willing to leave Your place of eternal glory, set aside your divine prerogatives, and become a man, a humble servant, to die the death that was due me. I hold tightly to many things in this world, but You didn't even hold tightly to being equal with God. Teach me to hold temporal things loosely, and to consider others more important than myself. Amen.

day 25

Paul's desire to share in the suffering of our Lord didn't come from a morbid interest in pain or misguided notion that suffering would somehow please God. He knew that sharing someone's experience is the best way to know him or her. He also understood that to know the Savior intimately will naturally result in becoming more like Him—having His patience and perseverance during suffering and, by His resurrection, sharing His victory over sin and death.

> . . . that I may know Him and the power of His resurrection and the fellowship of His sufferings, being conformed to his death.

> —Philippians 3:10

_____

_____

_____

_____

_____

_____

_____

_____

_____

_____

_____

_____

_____

Heavenly Father, I want to know the Lord Jesus in an intensely personal way that will affect who I am and all I do. Help me share everything that you have for me so that our fellowship can be very intimate and real. I yield myself to You. With each experience and every passing day, make me more like Christ. Amen.

Identification. Theologians use this term to describe a particular aspect of the believer's relationship with Jesus Christ: When Jesus died on the cross, you died. When Jesus was buried, you were buried. When Jesus rose from the dead, you rose. Just as Christ left His graveclothes behind, you left your life of sin in the grave. And the connection is, in some inexplicable way, more than merely symbolic. Consider the intimate nature of your relationship with God. How does it affect your relationship with the world?

> When you were dead in your transgressions and the uncircumcision of your flesh, He made you alive together with Him, having forgiven us all our transgressions, having canceled out the certificate of debt consisting of decrees against us, which was hostile to us; and He has taken it out of the way, having nailed it to the cross.
>
> —Colossians 2:13–14

Heavenly Father, Through the Cross, the code of the Law was cancelled, and we received new life in Christ. No longer enslaved, no longer condemned, forever identified and linked with Your Son. My heart now beats with Yours. Transform my perspective. Show me that I am foreign to the world around me. Give me wisdom and strength to live above it, just like Jesus. Amen.

Tetelestai! "It is finished!" This Greek term could apply to many things, including a task completed at work, but it has a much broader meaning. A priest, having found a sacrifice to be impeccable, would declare *tetelestai*. A merchant would stamp an invoice *satisfied, paid in full*. Upon release from prison, having served his time, a prisoner would receive a discharge document stamped *satisfied*.

Completed. Perfect. Satisfied. Accomplished . . . Finished.

No more work needs to be done; Jesus did it all. No more punishment required; He paid it all. No more wrath aimed at you, He took it all. Now rest.

> When He had made purification of sins, He sat down at the right hand of the Majesty on high.
>
> —Hebrews 1:3

_____

_____

_____

_____

_____

_____

_____

_____

_____

_____

_____

_____

_____

_____

_____

_____

_____

_____

_____

_____

_____

_____

_____

_____

_____

Father, Thank you that right now Jesus is seated next to You because He accomplished the work You sent Him to do. Thank you that because of Him, everything necessary for salvation has been completed. Now that I have placed my trust in Your Son and I rest upon His finished work, transform my mind to live accordingly. Amen.

Hollywood has made us lovers of suspense. Not knowing a plot's outcome enhances the thrill of watching a story unfold. Sometimes, though, it's good to know the ending of a story in advance. In the battle between God and the devil, we don't have to guess the outcome. We already know that God wins. When Jesus died on the cross, He defeated the devil and took away his power.

> Therefore, since the children share in flesh and blood, He Himself likewise also partook of the same, that through death He might render powerless him who had the power of death, that is, the devil.

> —Hebrews 2:14

_____

_____

_____

_____

_____

_____

_____

_____

_____

_____

_____

_____

_____

_____

_____

_____

Father, Thank you for sending Your Son to defeat Satan. Thank you that I don't have to fear death or the devil because Jesus took care of both. Help me to remember that You are in control of my future because of what Jesus did on the cross. Amen.

day 29

In the miracle of the Incarnation, the King of Glory laid aside Heaven's royal robes and clothed himself in the rags of humanity, with all its limitations: hunger, pain, fatigue, and loneliness. But God's act of becoming a man was no mere symbol of solidarity. He lived as we live—helpless while an infant, ignorant as a child, confused by adolescence, and as an adult, tried and frustrated and tempted. Throughout His life, He learned faithfulness through trial just as we do. And on the eve of His greatest temptation, He perfected obedience through blood-tainted sweat. The Father was pleased.

> Although He was a Son, He learned obedience from the things which He suffered.

—Hebrews 5:8

Almighty, Compassionate Father, I am so easily overcome by temptation in the weakness of my body. While I trust in the faithfulness of Your Son, Jesus, for my salvation, I long to feel Your pleasure by my obedience. But I am powerless even for that, so I look to Christ to please You through me. By the power of Your Spirit, take my trials, my suffering, and make me like Your Son—submissive, faithful, and obedient. Amen.

day 30

A will is a covenant with the deceased's survivors to ensure that they will receive everything due them. When someone writes a will, his or her wishes cannot be executed until he or she has passed away. The writer of Hebrews tells us that our covenant with Jesus is like a will. Because Jesus died, we can now enjoy what He promised to us: an eternal relationship with God with no need of a mediator. Jesus's death validated the covenant He made with us, so we can come to God confidently.

> For where a covenant is, there must of necessity be the death of the one who made it.
>
> —Hebrews 9:16

_____

_____

_____

_____

_____

_____

_____

_____

_____

_____

_____

_____

_____

Father, Thank you that Jesus's death on the cross opened the way for me to come to you any time and anywhere that I need to. I don't have to do anything or go to anyone else first; Your ears are always open to my prayers. And Your face is always turned toward me, Your child. Amen.

day 31

Do you realize the full implications of what Christ accomplished for you on the cross? By His sacrifice, Jesus has taken the sin issue between you and God off the table. Your sins are all forgiven—past, present, and future. Your sins cannot alter your relationship with your Father anymore. Your sins cannot separate you from your Father. Your sins cannot remove His tender love from you. Your sins cannot bring His justice upon you. Jesus Himself removed the sin issue, so that you might have unbroken, eternal, unlimited access to your Father.

> But now once at the consummation of the ages He has been manifested
> to put away sin by the sacrifice of Himself.

—Hebrews 9:26

_____

_____

_____

_____

_____

_____

_____

_____

_____

_____

My Father, I am awed by the completeness of what Jesus did for me on Calvary. To think that every sin I will ever commit has already been forgiven, and can no longer come between You and me. You have eternally cleared away whatever stood between us. I now have total and free access to You at any time. Oh Father, teach me to stand in the grace that is mine in Christ. Free me from thoughts of anything but love from You. Now that You have flung the door wide open, lead me into an ever-deepening communion with You. Amen.

On the day of Christ's crucifixion, a remarkable thing happened in the Temple in Jerusalem. In Israel's former days, in the temple's Most Holy Place, the eerie glow of God's special presence hovered above the symbol of the old covenant, the Ark. The holy chest contained Moses's stone tablets, representing the Law; a jar of manna, reminiscent of God's faithful provision; and Aaron's almond rod, affirming his authority to intercede as priest. A few feet away, a thick, heavy curtain shielded the people from a righteous, consuming holiness too dangerous to approach.

During earth's darkest hours, God's light hung on a tree just outside Jerusalem. The Law had been fulfilled, God's faithful provision had been confirmed, and the Great High Priest made holiness safe for humankind to approach. So, a veil no longer needed was torn open; for the man, Jesus, became the new way into God's presence.

> . . . by a new and living way which He inaugurated for us through the
> veil, that is, His flesh, . . .
>
> —Hebrews 10:20

_____

_____

_____

_____

_____

_____

_____

_____

_____

_____

_____

_____

_____

_____

_____

_____

_____

Awesome, Righteous God, I stand helpless and trembling before Your holiness, confident only in the provision of Jesus. Thank You, my Father, for making a way for me to come to You. Help me never to take the privilege lightly, yet never hesitate to approach. As You welcome me, may gratitude be my continual gift to You. Amen.

Ever wonder why war stories are so compelling? The warrior does the telling, so you already know the outcome: *victory*. Vivid details of agony and the struggle against impossible odds make the triumph all the sweeter as the warrior invites his hearers to savor the spoils. The story is a call to emulate the warrior and endure future battles with courage.

Jesus endured a cosmic battle that defeated sin and death. Now the author of Hebrews invites us to hear Christ's war story, take courage from the One who won the victory, and emulate His faithfulness.

> . . . fixing our eyes on Jesus, the author and perfecter of faith, who for
> the joy set before Him endured the cross, despising the shame, and has
> sat down at the right hand of the throne of God.

> —Hebrews 12:2

_____

_____

_____

_____

_____

_____

_____

_____

_____

_____

_____

_____

_____

_____

_____

_____

_____

_____

_____

_____

_____

_____

_____

_____

_____

_____

Almighty God, I praise You for Your awesome power and Your hatred of sin and death. Thank You for becoming one of us, and conquering evil on our behalf. I now submit to the control of Your Holy Spirit in me to persevere through trial, so that I may enjoy the victory celebration with You. Give me courage to follow Christ's example. Amen.

day 34

To a Jew, being sanctified, or set apart, gave him or her a strong sense of national and religious dignity. And it was costly. To go outside the camp of the Israelites was to enter into the world of the Gentiles, thus becoming ceremonially unclean. If one was forced out, he or she was considered to be "cut off from the land of the living."

Jesus turned sanctification on its head. According to Him, to be sanctified does not carry a special status or superiority with it; it means bearing disgrace and separation and mockery and death. It means carrying on our shoulders the same reproach that He bore when He went to the cross.

Are you willing to follow Him?

> Therefore Jesus also, that He might sanctify the people through His own blood, suffered outside the gate. So, let us go out to Him outside the camp, bearing His reproach. For here we do not have a lasting city, but we are seeking the city which is to come.
>
> —Hebrews 13:12–14

_____

_____

_____

_____

_____

_____

_____

_____

_____

_____

_____

_____

_____

_____

Father, May I, like the saints of old, confess that I am an alien and a stranger on earth. May I be willing to step outside the camp and bear the reproach that Jesus bore when He went to the cross for me, knowing that outside the comforts of the world, a better place has been prepared for me. Sanctify me, Father, and strengthen me. Amen.

day 35

There are few situations more discouraging than having to pay for wrongdoing that isn't your own. It is demoralizing to be misunderstood, distrusted, and penalized after making the right choices. A natural response might be to say, "Well, as long as I'm being punished, I may as well do as I please, even if it is wrong."

The apostle Peter has another perspective. Being a follower of Christ necessarily involves suffering as He suffered. And who was more innocent than He? Who endured more humiliation, more injustice than the perfect Son of God?

There's little dignity to be found in a beating that you deserve. Have courage. Trust God. He will turn your injustice into a badge of honor one day, and you can rest assured that the Holy Spirit will use your suffering to prepare you for greater joy with Him.

> For it is better, if God should will it so, that you suffer for doing what is right rather than for doing what is wrong. For Christ also died for sins once for all, the just for the unjust, so that He might bring us to God, having been put to death in the flesh, but made alive in the spirit.

> —1 Peter 3:17–18

Father, I hate being misunderstood. I don't understand a world that punishes the righteous and rewards the godless. Yet You allow it to continue. While I confess my inability to understand, I look to the example of Your Son to encourage and instruct me. I will remain faithful to do what is right by Your power despite the injustice. I trust that I will be vindicated one day, and that this experience will ultimately prove to be for my good. Amen.

day 36

A married couple who genuinely enjoys close fellowship will naturally have the same perspective on important matters—most especially on the issue of fidelity. If they don't, the marriage may prove to be a sham.

To walk in the Light is to have the mind of Christ. Not that we possess His intellect; He's omniscient! But if we truly believe in Him and have fellowship with Him, our perspectives will be the same—especially regarding sin. If not, we may have some serious self-evaluation to do.

Until we stand in Heaven, having received our new bodies, we will continue to struggle with sin and frequently fail. But the fact that we fail is no reason to doubt the genuineness of our relationship with Christ. The real question is: *Do you hate your sin?*

> If we say that we have fellowship with Him and yet walk in the darkness, we lie and do not practice the truth; but if we walk in the Light as He Himself is in the Light, we have fellowship with one another, and the blood of Jesus His Son cleanses us from all sin.
>
> —1 John 1:6–7

_____

_____

_____

_____

_____

_____

_____

_____

_____

_____

_____

_____

_____

_____

_____

Heavenly Father, Thank You for sending Your Son, Jesus, to die in my place. My gratitude for His sacrifice cannot be measured in words. Assure me by Your Spirit; help me to rest in the confidence that I am Yours. May I find sin as sickening and sorrowful as You do. Amen.

day 37

Many of us know that Jesus was a Jewish carpenter. We can imagine Him putting together a chair or even building a table, swinging a hammer and driving in nails. But can you picture Jesus in the courtroom . . . as a defense lawyer? The Bible says Jesus speaks in our defense—not because we are innocent and have been wrongly accused, but because we are guilty! And His defense? "Father, pour out Your wrath on Me."

> My little children, I am writing these things to you so that you may not sin. And if anybody sins, we have an Advocate with the Father, Jesus Christ the Righteous; and He Himself is the propitiation for our sins; and not for ours only, but also for those of the whole world.
>
> —1 John 2:1–2

_____

_____

_____

_____

_____

_____

_____

_____

_____

_____

_____

_____

_____

_____

_____

_____

Heavenly Father, I can almost imagine coming to the rescue of someone who has been wrongly accused, but You sent Jesus to come to the rescue of those who are guilty—people like me. Thank You for sending Jesus to stand in my defense. And thank You for sending Jesus to take my rightful punishment so that I may have a relationship with You. Amen.

day 38

Triumphant. Sovereign. King. Do these words enter your mind when you think of Christ beaten, scourged, and crucified? Jesus wasn't a victim of power-hungry leaders. He was and is the King above all kings who subjected himself to humiliation at the hands of men so that His own blood could set you free from your sins.

> . . . and from Jesus Christ, the faithful witness, the firstborn of the dead, and the ruler of the kings of the earth. To Him who loves us and released us from our sins by His blood . . .
>
> —Revelation 1:5

Lord, In the humanity of Your suffering and in the depths of Your sacrifice, You were also the Triumphant King and the Ruler above all men. Thank you, Lord, for the affliction You chose to endure, so that by the spilling of Your blood, I might be released from my sins. Help me to remember that You are sovereign above all circumstances and all men. Amen.

Have you ever felt guilty for not wanting to do something you know is God's will? For being tempted as strongly as you sometimes are? Do you ever think you should be above such feelings? Why? Jesus wasn't above them.

In the Passion sequence, today was the last day before Jesus entered Jerusalem. He knew He would die there. He spent the Passion Week in Jerusalem, knowing what was coming. And when the time came, in the Garden of Gethsemane, He prayed, "My Father, if it is possible, let this cup pass from Me. . . ." Yes, He chose to drink the cup. But at that moment *He didn't want to.* His humanity recoiled from it, just as ours does from some things God asks of us.

> He went away again a second time and prayed, saying, "My Father, if this cannot pass away unless I drink it, Your will be done."
>
> —Matthew 26:42

_____

_____

_____

_____

_____

_____

_____

_____

Father, I cannot relate to the magnitude of what You asked Your Son to do. But at times I, too, don't want to do what You ask. Gracious Father, in those times remind me that You don't ask me to feel like obeying You, but simply to obey. Grant me the strength to do so. And when I don't, remind me that because of what Jesus did on the cross, there is no condemnation for me. Amen.

On what we call Palm Sunday, Jesus entered Jerusalem riding a donkey colt. The crowd received Him as the conquering king that God had promised to King David a thousand years before, a descendant to sit on David's throne and establish an everlasting kingdom (see 2 Samuel 7:12–13). That was the meaning of their shouts, "Hosanna to the Son of David!" But Jesus wasn't the kind of king they expected. On this advent, He came to conquer sin and death, not Rome.

He came to bring us to God, so that we might make Him our greatest delight and become like Him. Jesus didn't come to make life on this earth comfortable, but rather to make us wholly His. He wants His kingdom, which one day will be physical, to be established in our hearts, here and now.

> The crowds going ahead of Him, and those who followed,
> were shouting,
>> "Hosanna to the Son of David;
>> Blessed is He who comes in the name of the Lord;
>> Hosanna in the highest!"
>
> —Matthew 21:9

_____

_____

_____

_____

_____

_____

_____

_____

_____

_____

_____

_____

_____

_____

Lord, You are the Promised One—He who is given an everlasting kingdom by the Father. Establish Your kingdom in my heart today. Show me where my agenda differs from Yours, and work in my heart so I might fully delight in what You delight: the Father and His will. Amen.

The palm branches had scarcely been removed from the previous day's celebration honoring the triumphant entry of a king when Jesus overturned the expectations of the money changers and merchants in the temple. With righteous indignation, He scoured the implements of empty worship and cast the profiteers aside.

Our preparations for the passion of Christ begin in earnest with a cleansing of our spiritual house. We can cast aside the vain offerings and empty sacrifices that were never asked of us. God desires a sacrifice of praise, and our humble prayers of confession bring glory to the Lord.

> [He said] to them, "It is written, 'And my house shall be a house of prayer,' but you have made it a robbers' den."

> —Luke 19:46

_____

_____

_____

_____

_____

_____

_____

_____

_____

_____

Lord, We pray that our lives will be free of the noisy clutter of distraction and compromise. Help us to cleanse the thresholds of our spiritual temple as we prepare to worship You in prayer today. Teach us to enter Your sanctuary and Your presence, which Jesus has made freely accessible to us. Amen.

day 42

Jesus taught about a realm beyond the material world: the spiritual world of God's kingdom. That's what made His words so captivating. He spoke of a world where oppressive rulers were not the ultimate authority (Luke 20:1–8), where justice is done (Luke 20:9–18), where people live forever with God (Luke 20:27–39), where humility, not earthly exaltation, is valued (Luke 20:45–47), where deeds are valued according to motive, not external show (Luke 21:1–4), and where righteousness would ultimately triumph and reign (Luke 21:5–36). His teaching was a message of hope for the downtrodden Israel—and for us today. His teaching challenges us to be transformed by God's Word and to see reality as God sees it, not as this world defines it.

> Now during the day He was teaching in the temple, but at evening He would go out and spend the night on the mount that is called Olivet. And all the people would get up early in the morning to come to Him in the temple to listen to Him.
>
> —Luke 21:37–38

_____

_____

_____

_____

_____

_____

_____

_____

_____

_____

_____

_____

_____

_____

_____

Holy Father, I am prone to thinking as this world thinks, to valuing what this world values, and to pursuing what this world pursues. Open my eyes to see as You see. Show me by Your Word and Your Spirit what is truly valuable, what You truly esteem, and what is truly eternal. Let me see myself and others as You see us, with Your eyes of love. And let me see that the satisfaction this world offers is an illusion which keeps my heart from being satisfied in You. Amen.

An alabaster jar filled with expensive perfume breaks gently in the feminine hands of a trusted friend. Mary, the sister of Lazarus, had once listened attentively at His feet (Luke 10:38–42), and had seen Jesus raise her brother from the dead (John 11:38–44). Now, Mary was pouring costly oil over Jesus's head.

Why? Hers was an offering born of gratitude, and Jesus recognized the fragrance of sacrifice laced with adoration. Mary freely gave so much, because she valued Jesus so highly. His preparation for the Cross had begun.

> But Jesus said, "Let her alone; why do you bother her? She has done a good deed to Me. . . . She has done what she could; she has anointed My body beforehand for the burial."

> —Mark 14:6, 8

Tender Lord, The expensive aroma of preparation fills our senses as we linger upon scenes of Jesus reclining at the Passover feast. Let me be motivated to bring an offering of preparation today, one that pierces my soul and reveals my grateful heart. Tomorrow is a day for last suppers and prayers in the garden, but today I need to muster my courage to absorb the sounds and scents of Your coming passion. May my appreciation for You grow as I fix my eyes upon Your sacrifice for me. Amen.

day 44 *Maundy Thursday*

The unleavened bread. The cups of wine. The shank of a lamb. The bitter herbs. These elements of the Passover meal tell a redemption story—how God freed the Hebrews from Egyptian bondage through doorways smeared with blood.

As Jesus celebrates the Passover the night before His death, He commemorates the past, and He inaugurates a new and better Passover. He breaks the bread of His own body; He offers the wine of His own blood; He lays down His life as the Lamb of God. The blood-smeared timbers of His cross would form the doorway to eternal life.

> When the hour came, Jesus and his apostles reclined at the table. And he said to them, "I have eagerly desired to eat this Passover with you before I suffer. For I tell you, I will not eat it again until it finds fulfill-ment in the kingdom of God."

> —Luke 22:14–16 (NIV)

_____

_____

_____

_____

_____

_____

_____

_____

Dear Father, I marvel at Jesus's eagerness as He offers Himself through the bread and wine. He savors the bitter herbs as they touch His lips. My redemption is a bitter task, yet He willingly accepts it. Thank You, Lord, for smearing Your blood on the doorposts of my heart—for willingly completing the Passover in me. Fill me with the same eagerness to serve You as You showed to redeem me. Amen.

The first blood of Christ's Passion was drawn not by a fist or a whip, but by a prayer. In Gethsemane, Jesus pleaded with His Father to take the cup of judgment from Him. So intense was Jesus's inner agony that sweat drops of blood dripped from His brow.

Only Jesus could bear the burden of God's judgment for sin—only Jesus. So in submission to the Father, He drew the wrathful cup to His lips. "Not My will, but Yours be done," He prayed as He received the will of the Father and the way of the Cross (see Luke 22:42).

Today, walk with Jesus through His final hours. Observe how His friend betrayed Him with a kiss. Watch His followers abandon Him; His most loyal soldier, Peter, deny Him; and His captors railroad Him through trials that brought Him to death. Even a vicious scourging didn't satisfy their thirst for His blood. Demanding that Jesus be put to death and disgraced, they chant in a frenzied chorus, "Crucify Him! Crucify Him!" Hear Pilate's order. See the soldiers lead Jesus away. Follow the Lamb to His slaughter.

When they came to the place called The Skull, there they crucified Him.

—Luke 23:33

Dear Father, As I gaze at Jesus on the cross, I scarcely comprehend that this day could be known as Good Friday. The good in Jesus's suffering was accomplished—for the world and for me. Thank you, Father, for handing Your cup of judgment to Your own Son. Thank You, Jesus, for receiving it and sacrificing Yourself for my sins. Amen.

The bleakest day of the disciples' lives was the day after Jesus's crucifixion. They had fled when Jesus was arrested. They remained in fearful hiding as late as Sunday night. In between, they had no hope. Their faith, their dreams, and their world had collapsed. Their Savior was gone.

Apart from Jesus's presence, we have no hope. We have no hope of being loved by a personal God. We have no hope of a relationship with God. We have no hope of eternal life. We have no hope that our lives in this tragic world are truly meaningful. As you anticipate tomorrow's celebration of the Resurrection, take a moment to consider where you would be, apart from Jesus. And give thanks to the Father for His astounding grace and mercy.

> Remember that you were at that time separate from Christ . . . having no hope and without God in the world.

> —Ephesians 2:12

My Father, Without Your reaching down and extending Your endless grace to me through Your Son, I had no hope in this life and eternity. I was separated from You and had no way to reach You. But because You loved me so much, You reached me. In the midst of life's trials, rejection by others, and my own failures, let me never forget how deeply and tenderly You love me. You are my hope, now and forever. Amen.

day 47 *Easter Sunday*

On the morning of the Resurrection, the warm rays of dawn's first light reveal an empty tomb. Jesus is risen! The darkness of death flees in the presence of the resurrected Christ—the One the prophets call, "the Sunrise from on high" (Luke 1:78).

The Passion story is not complete without the Resurrection. The Resurrection validates Jesus's death as effective for forgiving our sins. It enables us, through the Spirit, to live in power over sin. Christ's resurrection is our life.

> But now Christ has indeed been raised from the dead, the first fruits of those who are asleep.
>
> —1 Corinthians 15:20

_____

_____

_____

_____

_____

_____

_____

_____

_____

_____

_____

_____

_____

_____

_____

_____

_____

Dear Heavenly Father, If Jesus were merely a martyred hero, I would follow Him into death. But He is my living Savior! So I will follow Him into life! As a child of the Resurrection, I have no reason to fear death. Thank You, Father, for sending Your Son to die for me and to rise from the grave to live in me. Thank you for the promise of heaven that arches like a rainbow over Jesus's empty tomb. Amen.

INSIGHT FOR LIVING
DEVOTIONAL